How to Repair, Rebuild, and Restore Your Credit Score.

Dispute Letter Templates and Credit Repair Secrets Included so That You Can Take Action Today.

Tonette Stewart

Copyright © 2020 Queen Nette LLC

All rights reserved. No parts of this publication may be reproduced, stored in a retrieval system, or transmitted in any form other than personal use without the proper written consent of the author. Thank you for your support of the author's rights.

Disclaimer

This book should be used as a guide and educational tool to help you repair, rebuild, and restore your credit score yourself. Results vary based on individual credit, consistency and following proper timeframes of the dispute process. I nor can any credit restoration company guarantee you a perfect credit score or that all collections will be removed. However, from personal experience and positive client's results, I can assure you that these are the loopholes that are used. You should send all dispute letters certified mail so that you can acquire a tracking number. Allow 30 days for an update from all three major credit bureaus. Always attach a page or two of identifying documents that show your legal name and address such as driver's license, identification card or passport. Additional documents should be something with proof of a social security number like a paystub or W2. A copy of your credit report with the account in question highlighted is highly recommended. Your next round of dispute letters should be mailed on the 30th day of no response or within a couple days after receiving an unsatisfactory result. Please be advised that you will see fluctuations in your score during this process depending on the dispute results. During the repair process, try not to apply for any new credit and make sure to pay all bills on time. It's okay to apply for new credit during the rebuilding stage.

Please pay close attention to your mailbox during this process making sure not to miss out on any correspondence from the credit bureau or agency. These letters can be requesting further documents to complete your dispute claim. If not cleared during the allotted timeframe, your dispute can be dismissed. I can't emphasize enough how important it is to dispute derogatory marks by mail only. It will become very tempting to dispute these derogatory marks online, but you must follow the process and leverage your credit rights under the Fair Credit Reporting Act.

You are not reading this book by chance either. Someone or something in the universe believes that this guide is a major step to you reaching your financial goals. I want to congratulate you in advance on taking the time to educate yourself on how to repair, rebuild, and restore your credit. I thank you for trusting me. Now commit to trusting yourself!

I _____ am making this promise to myself on (date) _____ that I will not give up on myself and definitely not on this process. I understand that I cannot be upset with the results I do not get from the work I did not do.

Dedication to Page

To my son, Kairo. I'm building this legacy for you.

Table of Contents

Part 1

Introduction 3

Section 1: Selling Your Information for Profit 6

Section 2: You have to Know Your Credit Rights in Order to Fight! 8

Section 3: Derogatory Marks never looks Good 12
    Assignment #1 18

Part 2

Section 4: Top Five Ways to Increase Your Credit Score 27

Section 5: Credit Tips 34

Section 6: Bank vs Credit Union 36
    Assignment #2 39

Part 3

Section 7: Dispute Process Q & A 43

Section 8: Templates Explained 46
    Debt Verification Letter 53
    Cease & Desist Letter 57
    609 Letter 61
    30-day Follow Up Letter 65
    Goodwill Letter 69
    Credit Inquiry Letter 73
    Fraudulent Charge Letter 77
    Monthly Results Credit Tracker 83

Three Major Credit Bureaus & Contacts

Experian
P.O. Box 4500
Allen, TX 75013
1-888-Experian
www.experian.com

TransUnion Consumer Solutions
P.O. Box 2000
Chester, PA 19016-2000
1-800-916-8800
www.transunion.com

Equifax
P.O. Box 740241
Atlanta, GA 30374-0241
1-800-685-1111
www.equifax.com

About the Author

Three years ago, I remember writing three key credit steps on a piece of paper and handing it to a car sales client. After working with her for four hours, we both received a final response from the lenders that left us both drained. She was leaving without a car and me without a sale, but my heart felt for her because seven years ago, I was also a part of the poor credit score club. After looking at her credit, I knew that if she applied my advice; in 30 days, she could be approved for a reliable car and be on her way to good credit. Thirty-six days later, I was putting a big bow on her pre-owned certified 2016 Toyota Camry. Her smile was priceless. The feelings were mutual.

My name is Tonette Stewart and I created this guide with the intention to help you develop positive money habits, increase your credit score and your chances of reaching financial freedom. I wanted to make sure that I did so in a way that was simple, efficient and straight to the point. I grew up in Oakland CA and financial literacy was not a subject that was taught in school or at home. I was raised in an environment where responsibility wasn't a priority and instead of being able to enjoy my childhood, I was in constant survival mode.

Feeling like I only had two options; either survive by any means necessary or die trying to survive. I made the decision as an adolescent that I would create a better option not only for myself, but for those around me. I can honestly say that not becoming a statistic of child abandonment has been the hardest challenge of my life, but I have strategically used every job and opportunity to gain knowledge and life skills with the goal of passing it on to others. After working in the car sales industry and as a consultant for a successful credit repair company, I felt the dire need to create a guide that would not only educate but would help individuals with bad credit succeed.

Part 1

You Can't Successfully Change What You Don't Understand.

Part 1

Why Can't Successfully Change What You Don't Understand

Introduction

She felt her heart racing as her anxiety grew. She had been in this situation before but really needed this time to be different. She watched the sales consultant's lips as the disheartening words slowly released from her mouth. "I'm sorry. We tried but your auto loan was not approved. It's unfortunate but with your low credit score, the lenders declined your request." She slouched back in her seat, feeling defeated and tired. She was so sure that all the overtime hours she worked over the past few months for her down payment would be enough collateral to overlook her low credit score. She knew things had to positively change. She had to change. At that moment, she made the decision to repair her credit.

It's a known fact that having bad credit can have a huge impact on your life. It can be the deciding factor on the small decisions like cable or car insurance but a huge deciding factor on whether or not you get a higher paying job, a reliable automobile or housing. In situations where you are approved for a loan; a higher fee (interest rate) is charged which will ultimately put you in more debt.

Below is an example on exactly how much a small percentage in interest can result in a higher monthly payment and overall total cost on a used automobile.

- ❖ Excellent Credit - A $30,000 car at 3.0% interest for 72 months equals a monthly payment of $455 and a total cost of $32,818, with an interest fee of $2,818.
- ❖ Good Credit - A $30,000 car at 7.0% interest for 72 months equals a monthly payment of $511 and a total cost of 36,825. With an interest fee of $6,825
- ❖ Poor Credit – A $30,000 car at 15.0% interest for 72 months equals a monthly payment of $634 and a total cost of $45,673. With an interest fee of $15,673

Just by having a lower credit score, the associated increase in the interest rate can affect the overall lifetime cost of a loan. It is very important to educate yourself and understand the difference between Annual Percentage Rate (APR) and Annual Percentage Yield (APY). These two terms will be discussed in detail later in this manual.

Credit repair can be a daunting and time-consuming process which is usually the assumed reason why a lot of people would rather pay fees to a credit restoration company to do the legwork for them. However, during my credit consultant career, I realized that a lot of clients had the time but were paying for the services. The clients had no idea how or where to begin the process. They also didn't think that they could be successful at disputing negative items on their credit report and increasing their credit score. I created this guide so that you can.

Whether it is a medical bill, a repossession, late payments, bankruptcy, or student loans; all derogatory marks or debt can be removed from your credit report. You have to do your due diligence on the loopholes. However, not all debt is completely bad. In fact, in order to have excellent credit, you have to accumulate debt. It's the irresponsibility of managing debt that results in a bad credit score.

If you are expecting a 300-page book from an author that will overwhelm you with information, that either: (a) you will never use or (b) don't understand; then this is not the guide for you. If you are looking for something that will simplify the credit repair process, help increase your credit score and get you results; then congratulations, this is definitely the guide for you!

Let's make progress Not excuses.

Section 1: Selling Your Information for Profit

Just in case you haven't figured it out and still believe there are actual human beings who are controlling your credit score; let me be the first to tell you, there is not! Your information is being stored with a group of companies called Data Furnishers and these data furnishers make a profit off selling your information to the three major credit bureaus: Experian, Equifax and TransUnion. These companies then make billions of dollars by creating a credit score that is sold to third party companies. These third-party companies then use these scores to easily and quickly assess the risk of doing business with you.

Have you ever had to take an identity quiz and could not answer or remember the answers to the questions they asked you about yourself? I know me too, but the answer is actually really simple. Every time you release your personal information into the world, it is being stored for profit and will later be used against you. Think of all the fine print you didn't read when applying for a loan, employment, housing and even medical services. You just knew that you either needed or wanted these services so at that exact moment, you did not care. It is this exact thinking that keeps the working class working and 1% wealthy. **You did not read the fine print!**

Data furnishers are entities that have an agreement with a credit bureau to release personal information about their consumers. Information such as identity information, public records, credit accounts and anything you have ever applied to, even credit inquiries. The top furnishers are banks, lending institutions, credit card issuers and collection agencies. I know it's frustrating and you feel as if your privacy has been invaded. You're correct. However, the sooner you understand the system is not designed for everybody to win, the more you will pay attention to your actions, spending habits and how it will increase your overall credit score.

Section 2: You have to Know Your Credit Rights in Order to Fight!

"Formal education will make you a living; self-education will make you a fortune." –Jim Rohn

You may feel taken advantage of right now, but that is great. Hopefully, you use this ammunition I'm giving you to repair, rebuild, and restore your credit so that you're no longer the victim of credit declines, high interest rates, employment denials and even worse, lost housing opportunities. I want you to understand that you do have credit rights!

Consumers Protection Act (CCPA)

In 1968, several federal laws were enacted to assure that consumers would receive unbiased and honest credit practices. The CCPA assists the customer by:

- Helping to prevent identity theft by only putting the last five digits of a credit card number on store receipts.
- Requiring that fraud safety systems are put in place on your behalf that is designed to catch red flags to prevent identity theft.
- Requiring that the lender(s) take action when red flags arise even before a victim has been notified.

The Fair Credit Reporting Act (FCRA)

In 1970, the Fair Credit Reporting Act was enacted which helps regulate how consumer reporting agencies use your information. Under FCRA, you have rights that you should definitely be using to your advantage.

- You can download a free copy of all 3 of your credit reports once every 12 months or within the last 60 days of being declined for credit. You can access your most accurate credit reports 3 ways:
  - online: at AnnualCreditReport.com
  - phone: 877-322-8228 or
  - by mail
    - Annual Credit Report Request Service, P.O. Box 105281, Atlanta, GA 30348-5281

- You have the right to know what is in your "**File Disclosure.**" This file contains exact information on why you have been declined or denied employment, credit, or insurance due to your credit file. As a consumer you are entitled to a free disclosure every 12 months. This can be requested by phone at 877-322-8228.

- ❖ Your credit report should be 100% accurate! Credit bureaus are supposed to report verified information only. All inaccuracies such as fraud, unproven derogatory marks, misspelled names, addresses, etc., **can be disputed.**
- ❖ Your consent must be given in order for employers to access your credit report or any information
- ❖ If it makes you feel better, your credit report can only be sold to certain entities such as landlords, lending institutions, employers and insurance companies.

However, let's be honest! Once your personal information is stored, clever identity thieves can gain access.

- ❖ You have the right to freeze and unfreeze your credit report. This will stop creditors from being able to access your credit report and protect you from identity thieves being able to open new accounts. During this process you will setup a password that will give you the option to unlock it when you feel necessary. This can be done online or by calling directly to the credit bureau at:
  - ➢ **Equifax: 800-349-9960**
  - ➢ **Experian: 888-397-3742**
  - ➢ **Transunion: 888-909-8872**

❖ You have the right to "opt out" of these data collection bases and can do so by visiting OptoutPrescreen.com or call 888-567-8688. This will also stop all the marketing materials that flood your mailbox.

Credit Tip: Do your due diligence and look up LexisNexis and Innovis Data Solutions. These are also two major Data Furnishers that sell your information such as car and personal insurance claims, public records, and personal information for marketing purposes. Opting out can possibly help with your credit disputes but first request your C.L.U.E Report from LexisNexis. This can be done by phone, online or mail.

LexisNexis Risk Solutions
Website: www.optout.lexisnexis.com
Phone: 866-490-1920

Innovis Data Solutions
Website: www.optoutprescreen.com
Phone: 888-567-8688

Section 3: Derogatory Marks never looks Good

"Beware of little expenses; a small leak will sink a great ship." ~Benjamin Franklin~

There are some derogatory terms that you should become familiar with after you have downloaded your credit report. These negative items you will dispute using the template letters located at the end of this guide. Before you dispute anything, you **MUST** clear any misspelled names, addresses and phone numbers in the personal information section of your credit report. The only information that should be there is the correct spelling of your name, your current address and current phone number. This section is also used to verify accounts, so do not lessen your chances of a successful dispute process by skipping this step. The best results for removing your personal information is by phone.

All three of your credit reports will be different simply because not every credit bureau reports the same accounts. Experian is the most used credit bureau by lending institutions and the most difficult to get accurate (dispute). The reason most lending institutions use your Experian credit score to determine your eligibility is because they report all accounts.

Charge offs (C/O)

Charge offs can be confusing and can show up on your credit report under different scenarios. While working in the car sales industry, this is the one negative mark I most often witnessed. Charge offs seemed to appear on the majority of my customers that reported a total loss. A charge off is considered an unpaid debt and does not release you of the responsibility of the amount owed. A charge off means that the creditor has written off your debt but will continue to report the derogatory mark on your credit report for seven years. A creditor also has the option to sell the charge off to a collection agency which can become a complete nightmare for the customer.

Collections (COL)

If you have a collection showing on your credit report, this simply means that the original creditor sold your debt to a third-party company for profit. These third-party companies then do whatever is necessary to collect the entire amount due and sometimes add interest. Collections are the most common derogatory marks on a credit report. They usually appear on credit reports because of unpaid medical bills, credit cards, utility bills, and loans.

Repossession (RPO)

A repossession is a derogatory mark that appears on your credit report due to loss of property on a secured loan. This is most common on car loans where the lender will take back the vehicle and not refund you your previous payments. You are still legally responsible for the remaining amount of the loan.

Voluntary Surrender (VS)

A voluntary surrender is when you offer to return the property or vehicle due to non-payment. However, a voluntary surrender does not give you any special points. This has adverse consequences and impact on your credit score since you are defaulting on your loan and payment terms. This is still considered a repossession whether it's voluntary or not.

Foreclosures (FC)

Foreclosure is a term used when a homeowner has been evicted from their home due to unpaid mortgage of three months or more. Remember you're not technically a homeowner until you pay back the lender your full amount owed on your loan. Foreclosures are a derogatory mark that will have a huge negative impact on your credit. There are some alternatives to a foreclosure which includes a "short-term sale." Do your research on this type of sale. Short-term sales can have less negative impact on your credit report and may be more beneficial to your score in the long run.

Bankruptcy

Bankruptcy is a legal proceeding to request to be relieved from all debt obligations. Bankruptcy does negatively affect your credit score, yet depending on your personal circumstance, it may be a consideration. This derogatory mark can stay on your file seven to ten years depending on the type of bankruptcy filed. There are six types and are as follows:

- Chapter 7: Liquidation
- Chapter 9: Municipalities
- Chapter 11: Large Reorganization
- Chapter 12: Family Farmers
- Chapter 13: Repayment Plan
- Chapter 15: Used Foreign Cases

Chapters 7 & 13 are the most common bankruptcies filed for individuals, while Chapter 11 is the most common for business entities. For individuals, this legal proceeding can take anywhere from four months to five years, depending on which chapter is filed.

Late Payments

If you see a late payment reported on your credit report, that will hurt your credit score tremulously. Late payments are reported if your account is 30, 60 ,90 or 120 days past due. Just one late payment alone can decrease your score anywhere from 20 to 150 points depending on how many have been reported in the same cycle. The consequences of a low credit score include lower odds of credit approval, high interest rates on approvals, lower credit approval amounts, and longer repayment periods.

Debt Settlement

This is an agreement between you and the creditor where you agree to only pay back a part of the debt. This is not always the greatest idea unless in that same agreement you can include a **"pay to delete"** clause.

Students Loans

From personal experience, student loans can be tricky. After looking at thousands of credit reports during my car sales career, I've realized that some of the most affluent individuals are still in huge debt because of them. Although, student loans are one of the hardest debts to get discharged, it can be done. Proving undue hardship during a chapter 7 bankruptcy can cancel these loans. Occasionally, student loans can be canceled, discharged or even forgiven. Research on whether any of the programs listed below could work for you.

- ❖ Closed school discharge
- ❖ Teacher loan forgiveness
- ❖ Public Service loan forgiveness
- ❖ Perkin Loan Cancellation and discharge
- ❖ Unauthorized payment or False Certification of student eligibility

* Anytime you are looking to get an approval, whether it is a loan, credit card, automobile, housing or even a mortgage loan; the other key factor besides your credit score is your "**debt to income ratio**." They want to know if approved will you be able to manage the monthly payments?

The equation to calculate debt-to-income ratio is:

$$\frac{\text{Your Monthly Debt Payments}}{\text{Your Monthly Gross}} = \text{Debt to Income Ratio.}$$

Assignment #1

Let's Get Dispute Ready!

Your Current Credit Scores?

Experian _____ TransUnion _____ Equifax _____

How many negative accounts? _____

List names of negative accounts, amount & account number

1. _____
2. _____
3. _____
4. _____
5. _____
6. _____
7. _____
8. _____
9. _____
10. _____

How many total late payments?

_____

List names of open accounts with late payments

1. _____
2. _____
3. _____
4. _____
5. _____

List the names of closed accounts

1. _____
2. _____
3. _____
4. _____
5. _____
6. _____
7. _____
8. _____
9. _____
10. _____

How many total inquiries?
_____

List the agencies who performed inquiries

1. _____
2. _____
3. _____
4. _____
5. _____
6. _____
7. _____
8. _____
9. _____
10. _____

How many positive accounts?

_____

List the names of positive accounts

1. _____
2. _____
3. _____
4. _____
5. _____
6. _____

7. _____
8. _____
9. _____
10. _____

How many Credit Cards? _____

List credit card name, credit limit and APR

1. _____
2. _____
3. _____
4. _____
5. _____
6. _____
7. _____
8. _____
9. _____
10. _____

How many inaccurate names listed?

1. _____
2. _____
3. _____
4. _____
5. _____
6. _____
7. _____
8. _____
9. _____
10. _____

How many invalid addresses?

1. _____
2. _____
3. _____
4. _____
5. _____
6. _____
7. _____
8. _____

9. _____

10. _____

How many invalid phone numbers?

1. _____

2. _____

3. _____

4. _____

5. _____

6. _____

7. _____

8. _____

9. _____

10. _____

Do you feel more prepared?   YES ____ NO _____

Part 2
Information is Useless Unless You Apply It!

Section 4: Top Five Ways to Increase Your Credit Score

"Do the best you can, and don't take life too serious." ~Will Rogers~

During this process of repairing your credit, you will discover a lot of companies that offer to fix your credit for a fee. This is not necessarily a bad thing. Let's be honest, I am in the credit consulting business, myself. My company, Queen Nette LLC, and other firms offer services that can speed up the process of financial freedom for you and are great for individuals who don't have a lot of time to do the work themselves. I also understand that everyone doesn't have the financial resources to pay others, so that is exactly why I created this guide for you to do it yourself. My passion as an entrepreneur is to authentically help those who want to help themselves.

Here is your Top 5: Do Your Due Diligence

1. Become an authorized user

This particular option includes having access to someone who trusts you, pays their bills on time and want to help you succeed. If done correctly, it can boost your credit 75+ points in 30 days **without any risk** to the original card holder. This works so quickly because you will gain access to their credit history which includes their positive payment history.

The original card holder simply contacts their credit card company and advises them to add you as an authorized user. Depending on the credit card company, they may need your social security number, date of birth and other identifying information so that they can properly report to your credit bureaus. Once the card arrives, they will simply activate the card for you and shred it.

2. A Secure Card

A secured card is very similar to an unsecured card. You can get positive payment history reported which will help increase your credit score. Make sure you ask and are aware of which credit bureaus that particular card reports to so that you have a clear understanding on which credit bureau(s) to check.

Understand that most (but not all) secured cards require

a minimum deposit of $200 dollars but will allow you to load up to $2,000. This is an important factor because some secure cards have a probation period where the company will not allow you to increase your original deposit amount for 90+ days.

If you need a secure card it's for one of two reasons: (a) you don't have any credit and the credit bureau(s) want to see how you handle your own money before they lend to you or (b) you have challenged credit and made some bad decisions and now you have to regain the trust of the with the agencies that gave you a chance.

A secure card is a great way to start and rebuild credit. As a disclaimer, I am in no way telling you which ones to apply for but simply giving you information on what I have seen work. I have listed some card options on the following page:

- **The Discover it Secured– No Credit Check**
  - Offers cash back rewards!
  - Minimum deposit of $200
  - No Annual Fee
  - Reports to all three major credit bureaus
- **First Progress Platinum - No Credit Check**
  - Minimum of $200 deposit (Refundable)
  - Annual fee of $29.00
  - Reports to all three credit bureaus
- **OpenSky - No Credit Check**

- Requires a deposit of a minimum $200 The more you can deposit, the better it will look on your credit report.
- Annual fee of $35.00
- Reports to all three major credit bureaus

❖ **Applied Bank Secured Card**
- Requires minimum of $200 deposit and maximum of $1,000. You can increase your limit up to $5,000 at any time after the initial deposit
- Interest rate is set at one of the lowest, I've seen for a secure card at a fixed 9.99% meaning it will always stay the same.
- Report to all three major credit bureaus

❖ **Capital One Mastercard** –
- Minimum deposit of $49, $99 or $200
- No Annual Fee
- Reports to all three major credit bureaus

❖ Bonus: **Credit One Card**
- One of the only unsecured card that you can get with poor credit! 90% approval odds with bad credit

Get pre-qualified on their website first!
www.creditonebank.com

3. Credit Boosting & Positive Tradelines

You don't always have to apply for a credit card to help increase your credit score. However, eventually you will need a mixture of a few credit cards to continue your journey to attain excellent credit. You will come across a lot of financial institutions that will offer a range of credit building tools for a monthly fee. The one I currently use is Experian Boost. It's Free!

- ❖ This will only work if you pay your monthly bills through a bank account. Simply connect the qualified account through the Experian website.
- ❖ This service lets you get credit for paying utility bills, cell phone bills and even streaming service bills like Hulu and Netflix. However, please do your research for more information.
- ❖ There are also ways to obtain positive tradelines by simply paying your rent every month. Your landlord or rental property manager can simply do this for free but 99% of the time, you may have to inquire, or request payments be reported to credit bureaus.

Other companies may charge a fee like Credit My Rent, but they will go back as far as two years of positive payment history which is amazing.

4. Credit Builder Loans

Credit builder loans are not loans you hear about often, but they do exist. These easy approval loans are usually only offered through credit unions and don't require you to have a good credit score. As with everything else, I mention in this book, please do your research.

- ❖ These non-traditional loans are used as a savings accounts where you get a positive reporting history by paying yourself. After you reach your loan goal, the money then becomes available to you.
- ❖ If you don't have a credit union, there are many online companies that offers this loan such as SELF and MoneyLion.
- ❖ Jewelry Stores are the easiest to get a small loan even with bad credit. Financing a small piece of jewelry and paying it off in six months can boost your credit. Always ask for the approval requirements but small companies like Prestigio have guaranteed credit approvals.

5. Balance Transfer Cards

Did you know that there are cards where you can consolidate debt to one card, get rid of your high interest rates and have a new APR of 0% up to 18 months? Please do your due diligence on which card will work best for you.

- ❖ Citi Double Cash Card
- ❖ Citi Diamond Preferred
- ❖ Discover it
- ❖ U.S. Bank Visa
- ❖ Bank Americard

Credit Unions usually will have the best options of balance transfer cards for challenged credit and easier approval odds!

*Bonus: Debt Consolidation

Debt consolidation is the process of rolling multiple debts into one payment. It's usually used for high interest debt like credit card bills. Debt consolidation can help you pay off your debt in a faster and more organized manner. However, it could help or hurt you depending on the option you choose. Do your due diligence on the best option for your particular situation.

Section 5: Credit Tips

The most difficult thing is the decision to act, the rest is merely tenacity." ~Amelia Earhart~

These are tips but please take them seriously. They can make or break your credit repair process!

1. Do Your Research! What may work for someone else may not work for you.
2. 35% of your credit score is Payment history. Pay all your bills on time, if possible early.
3. Set up as many automatic payments possible. This feature reduces the chances of late payments.
4. 30% of your credit score is owed debt pay down strategically. Focus on the highest interest rate debts, first.

5. 15% of your credit score is credit history. The longer the credit history, the better. This helps lenders decide on offering new lines of credit.
6. 10% of your credit score is new credit. Please be strategic when applying for new credit.
7. Have a credit mixture. This is another 10% of your score (credit card, charge card, car loan, etc.)
8. Ask for a credit limit increase on open accounts.
9. Do not close unused credit card accounts. This will also delete all your positive payment history and credit history on that particular account.
10. Decrease and maintain your utilization of credit cards to 30%.
11. If you have a high interest rate car loan, REFINANCE!
12. Dispute! Dispute! Dispute any inaccuracies!
13. Do not just pop your letters in the corner mailbox. Mail your letters certified.
14. Don't take no for an answer, if needed, dispute again!
15. Check your credit score regularly

*Following the dispute process exactly as I have described it in this book. Remember, these results are based around response time (30 days is important)!

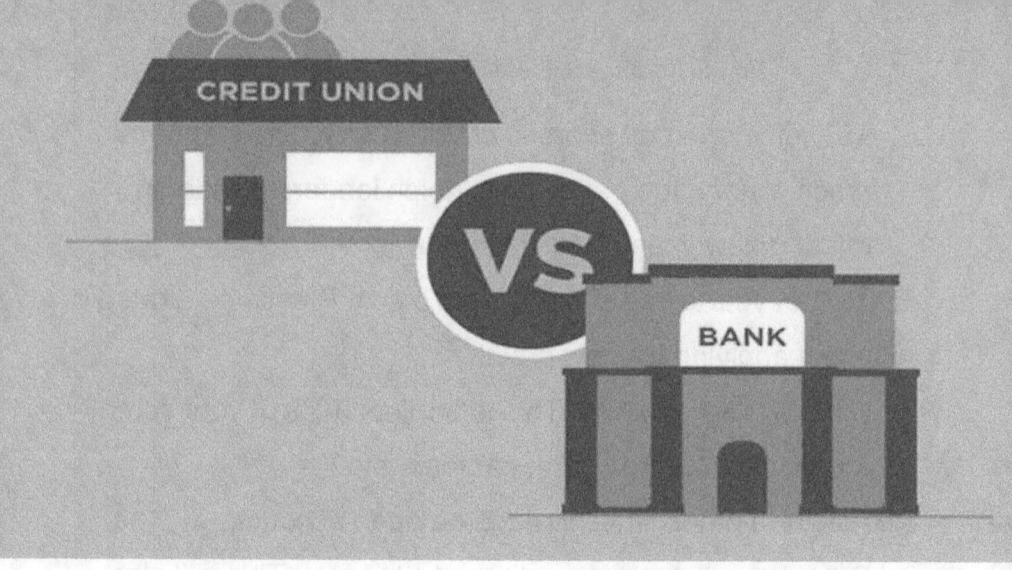

Section 6: Bank vs Credit Union

"Many folks think they aren't good at earning money, when what they don't know is how to use it." –Frank A. Clark

In this section, you will notice that I will frequently use the term "annual percentage yield" (APY). Just in case you do not know this term, it is defined as the percentage that your deposit could earn in one year. There are several different entities that use this calculation for your savings, money market and checking accounts.

Banks

A bank is a for profit financial institution. For profit means that the company makes profit off lending the money that you deposit into the bank to other borrowers. They give what is called an incentive APY of 0.01% to 0.05% depending on the balance in your account. The bank will then charge a higher interest rate to the borrowers. The profit from lending your money at a higher interest rate is called "interest income."

Banks offer a huge range of services and usually have tons of locations worldwide, so they tend to be convenient. They are considered a one-stop shop for all things financial like checking accounts, business accounts, trust funds, retirement plans and more. They give you easy access to your money with so many locations and ATMs you can usually find two or more locations per city.

Credit Unions

Credit Unions are nonprofits meaning that they are organizations cooperatively owned by their members. These financial institutions are run by a board of volunteers who are also members. Their goal is to help their members save more by keeping low loan interest rates and low fees, while maintaining a high APY on savings accounts. The interest rates on your credit union accounts range anywhere from 0.20% - 4.09% APY and ever higher on investment accounts.

To become a member, you typically have to meet certain criteria for that specific credit union. Examples of this are live, worship or work within a certain location. There are many employers that sponsor certain credit unions. Do your research on if your employer recommends one. I personally started to take a closer look at credit unions while working in the car sales industry. It seemed like all my clients that had good to excellent credit were members of credit unions. They would have the lowest interest rates and if they did decide to put down a down payment or pay in full, it was straight from their credit union account. After doing my due diligence I opened a credit union account of my own, I was surprised by all the perks I received just by being a member. These perks included:

- Free Savings Account
- Lowest Auto Loan Rates
- Low Mortgage Loans rates
- Free Notary Services
- Guaranteed Auto Refinancing
- Free Coin Exchange
- Access to a low interest rate balance transfer card
- Free Credit Workshops

Do your own research on the credit union that works best for you. You can also research and find that there are credit unions who offer the same services as traditional banks such as business accounts and business loans.

* It is safe! Although, credit unions are nonprofit, your money is insured by the National Credit Union Administration.

Assignment #2

Is your Money Growing or Shrinking?

I am a strong believer that every dollar counts especially when you are saving for a goal. As a credit consultant, the questions I am often asked by clients is "should I become a member of a credit union?" I believe that it is a great idea, but that is just my opinion. I'll let you make that decision. After completing this assignment, you should be able to determine whether the bank account you have works or if changes need to be made. What is the interest earning (APY) on your savings account?

_____

Do your current accounts have a monthly maintenance fee?
_____

Is there a minimum monthly balance required and fee?
_____

Are there any free services you receive for banking there? (free notary, etc.)
_____

What is the interest rate on your savings account?
_____

How much are overdraft fees?
_____

What services do they offer for challenged credit? (ex. Secure cards, workshops, balance transfer cards.)
_____

Stop payment fees? (if you cancel a payment)
_____

Notes

Part 3

80% of Consumers Who Dispute Credit Errors are Successful.

Part 3

Section 7: Dispute Process Q & A

1. **What is the Credit Dispute Process?**

    It's the process of increasing your credit score by correcting all inaccurate information. The process includes making a dispute to the reporting credit bureaus which can be done by Phone, Mail or Online.

2. **Does Making a Credit Dispute hurt your Credit?**

    Absolutely not, but depending on the results of the dispute your scores can change. For example, if you dispute a medical bill currently in collections and it results in a deletion, then your score will increase. However, if you're disputing identification inaccuracies such as names, addresses etc., it will stay the same because correcting this information has no impact on credit.

3. **Can I get in trouble for disputing accurate information?**

The Fair Credit Reporting Act gives everyone the right to dispute any information listed on credit report in which you don't agree. You make the decision on what and how to dispute.

4. **How long does the dispute process take?**

Dispute results will be different for everyone. It will all depend on your personal credit report and exactly what type of derogatory marks are reported. You can see an increase as early as 30 days.

5. **Should I discuss a dispute with an agency over the phone?**

No all conversations are recorded any admission of guilt will be used against you. It's best to get all interactions on paper or by email.

6. Will my credit be wiped clean after seven years?

Not exactly. All positive accounts will remain, but any unpaid debt should fall off seven years after the original negative report date.

7. How long does it take to get a dispute response?

Anywhere from 7 to 45 days pending on which method you dispute the inaccuracies. After 30 days of no response according to the FCRA, the inaccuracies should be deleted.

8. What should I do if my dispute is denied?

Dispute again but this time attach a 100-word consumer statement to explain your position and why you feel the decision is incorrect.

9. What is a FICO Score?

The Fair Isaac Corporation (FICO) is a credit reporting tool based on the specific type of loan you are applying. We all have multiple FICO scores (i.e. Auto, Insurance, Mortgage).

Section 8: Templates Explained

Depending on your personal credit report, the process of disputing your derogatory marks by mail will take a lot of envelopes; so, buy a box. You will need to send separate letters to separate credit bureaus so make sure that each letter is tailored as such.

Debt Validation Letter

This letter is a valuable during your debt collection process. Use this letter to request how much is owed, documents that prove you owe, who the debt is owned and for collection proceedings not to continue until proof of validation is completed.

Cease and Desist Letter

Creditors and collection agencies can become aggressive and relentless when attempting to collect a debt they believe is owned. This is the letter you want to use to stop all harassment calls, letters, and emails.

609 Letter

This particular letter is what you want to use when you want to request a removal of any inaccurate or accurate information. Under the 609 Fair Credit Reporting Act, you have the right to request to remove both simply because credit bureaus have a responsibility to only report VERIFIED information. The reason this particular letter has success is because it requests that the creditor provide the original signed copy of your application which makes it very difficult to verify.

30-day Follow Up Letter

This letter is needed if the credit bureau has not responded within 30 days.

Goodwill Letter

Everyone makes mistakes and it's always easier to simply ask for forgiveness when you have owned up to your mistakes and have been working hard to correct them. This letter is a tool used on current, open accounts that now have a positive payment history. It's called a goodwill letter because you are asking the credit to remove the derogatory marks that resulted from late payments from your credit report and to empathize with you. If late payments are showing up on your credit report incorrectly, this letter should not be used but instead disputed.

*Trick- If you email this letter directly to the CEO of the company, you not only have a greater chance of getting them removed, but a faster result! (send it in email form, **NOT** as an attachment)

EX. Google "CEO of Santander Consumer USA"

Email: Maditya@santanderrconsumerusa.com

Credit Inquiry Removal Letter

Removing inquiries from your credit report will give you a credit score increase. There are two types of inquiries: hard inquiries and soft inquiries. Hard inquiries result from you giving your legal permission for your credit report to be accessed in order to determine your qualification. Car loan, mortgage, credit card or loan companies pull hard inquiries. Soft inquiries are accumulated by a company accessing your credit to see if you meet the basic requirements for any pre-approval offers.

Identity Theft/ Fraudulent Charge Letter

In today's society, many people are not only losing their employment but also their homes due to an unpredictable economy. Identity theft is at an all-time high and folks are suffering from their personal information being sold on the dark web or landing in the hands of the wrong people. Unfortunately, someone can completely ruin your credit and steal your earnings way quicker than the lifetime it took for you to build it. There are many companies like LifeLock that offer credit monitoring services for a fee. They are designed to give people a peace of mind; yet, as with other things in life, unfortunately this is not a 100% guaranteed. Recovering from identity theft can be a very difficult and long process but it can be done. This letter should be accompanied by a police report showing that you did file a legal claim that your identity was indeed stolen.

Dispute Result Terms

Once the three major credit bureaus have finished with their investigation of your disputes, they will send you a packet. This packet will contain the accounts you disputed and the results of those particular accounts. The result terms will be as follows:

Frivolous Claim

If this appears on your investigation report, it simply means that you either filed a duplicate dispute or you didn't include enough information in the original dispute. This can be a missing account number, missing identifying documentation, etc.

Deleted

It means just that the derogatory mark has been removed from your credit report. However, a deleted item can reappear on your credit report this is called "**reinsertion**."

Remember that the way the dispute process works is if the credit bureau is unable to verify that the information is correct or respond within 30 days, then it must be deleted and removed. Still, there is what I like to call a five-day grace period in which you have to be notified if the data furnisher discovered that the information was indeed verified and accurate.

You can dispute again, but I would make sure that you try a different approach by submitting a little more proof on why it's inaccurate or a 100-word statement. This statement is a letter that would be stored in your credit file and anyone who has access may be able to see it. I would be careful of what type of information is submitted to make sure there is no admission of guilt that could be used against you during a different dispute.

Updated

This means that the information has been updated.

Verified/Remain

The data furnisher has reported to the credit bureau that the information is accurate and will remain as is on your credit report.

* Credit Karma is not an accurate reflection of your credit scores. However, it is free and is an absolute great tool to use for credit alerts, collections and any fraudulent activity that may possibly occur. The reason it is not an accurate reflection is because it is based off of your

Transunion credit report and their credit scoring system.

Notes

Debt Verification Letter

*Bold Face wording should not be changed but please input necessary information inside the parentheses ( ).

Debt Verification Letter

[Current Date]

[Your Name]
[Your Address]

[Debt Collector's Name]
[Debt Collector's Address]

Re: [Your Account Number]

To Whom It May Concern,

This letter is in response to notice I, [Your Name], received on [Date of Contact] of a owed debt. **In accordance with 15 U.S. Code § 1692g,** I am requesting proof that I am indeed the responsible party of this debt, including the age of the debt, an itemized statement of what is owed, the name and address of the original creditor, and evidence of contractual agreement that I have a legal obligation to pay you.

Please consider this debt to be under dispute. If it is found that there is no evidence of this debt under my name, then I request that all credit bureaus and appropriate financial institutions be made aware or a complaint will be filed to the respective local or federal agency.

I am aware of the request for payment by your company and any further telephone communication shall be considered harassment in violation of 15 U.S. Code § 1692d and shall be subject to State and Federal penalties.

Thank you for your cooperation, and I look forward to your response.

Sincerely,

[Your Signature]

Cease & Desist Letter

***Bold Face wording should not be changed but please input necessary information inside the parentheses ( ).**

Cease & Desist Letter

[Date]

[Full Name]
[Full Address City, State Zip]

[Collection Agency]
[Collection Agency Address City, State Zip]

RE:[Account Number]

Dear [Collection Agency],

This letter serves as a notice that I am exercising my right to request under the **Fair Debt Collection Practices Act Section 805 (C), that you immediately CEASE and DESIST all contact with me.** With this notice, under the law, you can now only contact me at: [preferred email address]

To advise me that your company's further efforts are being terminated;

To notify me that your company may invoke specified remedies which are ordinarily invoked by such debt collector or creditor; or

Where applicable, to notify me that your company intends to invoke a specified remedy.

GIVE THIS LETTER THE IMMEDIATE ATTENTION IT DESERVES.

Sincerely,

[Your Signature]

609 Letter

*Bold Face wording should not be changed but please input necessary information inside the parentheses ( ).

609 Letter

[Your Name]
[Your Address]
[Phone #]

[Date]

Subject: Fair Credit Reporting Act, Section 609

Dear [Experian, TransUnion, or Equifax]

I am exercising my right under the Fair Credit Reporting Act, Section 609, to request information regarding an item that is listed on my consumer credit report: (Ex. 411 Collection Agency, account number 0123456789).

As per Section 609, I am entitled to see the source of the information, which is the original contract that contains my signature.

My identifying information is as follows:
Date of Birth: [01/21/1989]
SSN: [123-45-6789]

As proof of my identity, I have included copies of my (birth certificate OR Social Security card, passport OR driver's license, rental agreement, OR a cellphone bill). I have also included a copy of my credit report with the account I am requesting to have verified circled and highlighted.

If you are unable to verify the account with the original contract, the information should be removed from my credit report within 30 days.

Sincerely,

[Signature]

30-day Follow Up Letter

*Bold Face wording should not be changed but please input necessary information inside the parentheses ( ).

30-Day Follow Up Letter

[Date]

[Your Name]
Your Address City, State Zip]

[Credit Bureau]
[Credit Bureau Address City, State Zip]

RE: Dispute Letter (date of first letter)

Dear (Experian, Equifax, or TransUnion),

This letter is a formal notice that you have failed to respond to my dispute letter that was sent on (DATE). This letter was mailed certified and I have enclosed a copy of the receipt which you signed on (DATE). As you are aware, federal law requires you to respond within 30 days which currently has exceeded this period. I know you are aware that failure to comply with federal regulations put in place by credit reporting agencies are in serious violation of the Fair Credit Reporting Act and may be investigated by the FTC. I am maintaining detailed records of all my correspondence with you.

It seems that you may have misplaced my letters or failed to respond due to the high volume of dispute requests you receive daily. If this is the case, I'm sure you'll want to handle this particular matter as soon as possible. To make it easier, I've included a copy of my original request, the dated receipt of your reception of the original letter and a copy of the proof verifying the validation of the credit item you have mistakenly placed on my records.

The following information requested per dispute letter therefore needs to be verified and deleted from the report as soon as possible.

Sincerely,

[Your Signature]
Last 4 SSN# [xxxx]

Goodwill Letter

***Bold Face wording should not be changed but please input necessary information inside the parentheses ( ).**

Goodwill Letter

[your name]
[your address]

[date]

Account Number: [your account number]

[Credit Card Company]
[Credit Card Company Address City, State Zip]

To Whom It May Concern:

I am aware that you may have a high volume of requests and want to first thank you for taking the time to read my letter. I'm writing because I noticed that my most recent credit report contains [a late payment/ payments] reported on [date/dates] for my [name of account] account.

I understand that it is my responsibility to pay my financial obligations on time, and if it weren't for [circumstance that caused you to miss a payment], I'd have an excellent repayment history. I made a huge mistake in falling behind, but since then, [description of how your circumstances have changed or how you've improved your money management]. As you can see, I've had a 100% on-time payments history.

I'm planning to apply for [a mortgage/auto loan/etc.], and after doing my research, I realize that the missed payment on my record could hurt my ability to qualify. I believe that this record doesn't reflect my creditworthiness and commitment to repaying my debts. It would help me tremendously if you could give me a second chance and make a goodwill adjustment to remove the late [payment/payments] on [date/dates].

Thank you for your consideration, and I hope you'll approve my request.

Sincerely,

[Signature]

Credit Inquiry Letter

***Bold Face wording should not be changed but please input necessary information inside the parentheses ( ).**

Credit Inquiry Letter

(Name)
(Address, City, State, Zip Code)

(Social Security Number)
(Date of Birth)

(Today's Date)

(Credit Report Dispute Department)
(Credit Bureau Name)
(Street Address, City, State, Zip Code)

To whom it may concern,

This letter is to dispute an unauthorized inquiry on my credit report. On (insert date of report), I retrieved a copy of my credit report (insert credit report number) and discovered an inquiry that I have no knowledge of. I did not apply for credit with (insert creditor or lender), I have also reached out asking that they remove the inquiry from my credit profile.

I'm asking you to please launch an investigation into (creditor's name) inquiry to determine who authorized it. Upon completion, please provide written correspondence that details the results of your findings.

If you find that the inquiry is invalid, I am requesting that it be removed from my credit report as soon as possible. But if (creditor's name) is able to prove that the inquiry is indeed valid, please provide written proof and a description of how the investigation was conducted.

Thanks in advance for your prompt attention to this matter.

Sincerely,

(signature)

Fraudulent Charge Letter

*Bold Face wording should not be changed but please input necessary information inside the parentheses ( ).

Fraudulent Charge Letter

[Date]

[Your Name]
[Your Address]
[Your City, State, Zip Code]

[Name of Creditor]
[Fraud Department (companies may specify an address to receive fraud dispute letters), or Billing Inquiries Department]
[Address]
[City, State, Zip Code]

[RE: Your Account Number (if known)]

Dear [creditor name]:

I am writing to dispute a fraudulent charge that I noticed on my billing statement in the amount of $____. I am a victim of identity theft, and therefore not responsible for this charge that I did not make or authorize. I am requesting that the charge be removed, that any finance/ other charges related to the fraudulent amount be credited, and that I receive an accurate statement. **This request is made pursuant to the Fair Credit Billing Act's amendments to the Truth in Lending Act, 15 U.S.C. §§ 1666-1666b, 12 C.F.R. § 226.13. See also 12 C.F.R. § 226.12(b).**

Enclosed are copies of [use this sentence to describe any enclosed information, such as sales slips, payment records] supporting my position. Please investigate this matter and correct the billing error as soon as possible.

Sincerely,

[Your Name]

KEY Credit Repair Terms

```
D R I A P E R T I D E R C I U Z M O Y Y
Q B G V F A D Y T U A S Z H F Q D N Y C
L Q D R P Z A R C F E W E T Y S G M X R
J X E H I N T T R I B I T A I F J Q E E
P Q I P O Q A T R N R D U K S N R P H D
L N F E C S F I V U E E P O D R U S S I
Z Z I I I E U K N Q W U S J B S W L W T
M D R A F Q R A C G P O I Z C L F M Z S
R J E J N W N N E X O R D Q K A X A M C
G F V I G V I A S R M O F U J T Y G D O
H F H F Q E S E B W U H X X C E B S Y R
I N C O M E H Y T U E B S E K P J E Q E
T D R E S U E Z I R O H T U A A F T D Q
X V V D S I R X N X D R Y I E Y L T D Z
X P Y A Y S E C U R E C A R D M J B I D
V C D E T A D P U W T X J F N E S X A P
O O X L E N U Q O U E C F G M N R F J L
Y G C N T U A I Q U L U K C T T F C L J
U S W F V U V F M X E Z J B G S V P P G
K V T V K Q D C H N D V J T N T Y Y U J
```

CREDIT BUREAUS
CREDIT REPAIR
CREDIT SCORE
FICO
INQUIRIES
LATE PAYMENTS
SECURE CARD
DATAFURNISHER

FCRA
AUTHORIZE USER
DEBT
INCOME DELETED
UPDATED
VERIFIED
DISPUTE

I'm so proud of you! Thank you for your support I'm excited for you to take everything you have learned and apply it to you repairing your credit. Remember:

1. You can't change what you don't understand.
2. Your credit report should be 100% accurate!
3. Cash is king but credit holds conversations.
4. 80% of consumers who dispute credit report errors are successful.
5. In order to get your credit in order your finances need to be in order.
6. Information is useless unless you apply it!
7. Bad credit won't fix itself.
8. An 800 Credit Score has more purchasing power than $100,000.
9. Set up as many automatic payments as possible.
10. There are only two options make progress or make excuses.

Monthly Results Credit Tracker

*Use These Monthly Sheets to Track Your Credit Score Results.

Month 2 Results

❖ **Your current score**

_____

❖ **Did it increase or decrease?**

_____

❖ **How many points?**

_____

❖ **What accounts responded?**

_____

❖ **What was the result?**

_____

Month 3 Results

❖ **Your current score**

_____

❖ **Did it increase or decrease?**

_____

❖ **How many points?**

_____

❖ **What accounts responded?**

_____

❖ **What was the result?**

_____

Month 4 Results

❖ **Your current score**

_____

❖ **Did it increase or decrease?**

_____

❖ **How many points?**

_____

❖ **What accounts responded?**

_____

❖ **What was the result?**

_____

Month 5 Results

- **Your current score**

  _____

- **Did it increase or decrease?**

  _____

- **How many points?**

  _____

- **What accounts responded?**

  _____

- **What was the result?**

  _____

Month 6 Results

❖ **Your current score**

_____

❖ **Did it increase or decrease?**

_____

❖ **How many points?**

_____

❖ **What accounts responded?**

_____

❖ **What was the result?**

_____

Month 7 Results

❖ **Your current score**

_____

❖ **Did it increase or decrease?**

_____

❖ **How many points?**

_____

❖ **What accounts responded?**

_____

❖ **What was the result?**

_____

Month 8 Results

❖ **Your current score**
_____

❖ **Did it increase or decrease?**
_____

❖ **How many points?**
_____

❖ **What accounts responded?**
_____

❖ **What was the result?**
_____

Month 9 Results

❖ **Your current score**

_____

❖ **Did it increase or decrease?**

_____

❖ **How many points?**

_____

❖ **What accounts responded?**

_____

❖ **What was the result?**

_____

Month 10 Results

❖ **Your current score**

_____

❖ **Did it increase or decrease?**

_____

❖ **How many points?**

_____

❖ **What accounts responded?**

_____

❖ **What was the result?**

_____

Month 11 Results

- ❖ **Your current score**

  _____

- ❖ **Did it increase or decrease?**

  _____

- ❖ **How many points?**

  _____

- ❖ **What accounts responded?**

  _____

- ❖ **What was the result?**

  _____

Month 12 Results

❖ **Your current score**
　　_____

❖ **Did it increase or decrease?**
　　_____

❖ **How many points?**
　　_____

❖ **What accounts responded?**
　　_____

❖ **What was the result?**
　　_____

www.ingramcontent.com/pod-product-compliance
Lightning Source LLC
LaVergne TN
LVHW051508070426
835507LV00022B/2983